CENGAGE Learning

Novels for Students, Volume 32

Project Editor: Sara Constantakis Rights Acquisition and Management: Beth Beaufore, Leitha Etheridge-Sims, Jackie Jones, Kelly Quin Composition: Evi Abou-El-Seoud Manufacturing: Drew Kalasky

Imaging: John Watkins

For product information and technology assistance, contact us at **Gale Customer Support, 1-800-877-4253.**

For permission to use material from this text or product, submit all requests online at **www.cengage.com/permissions**.

Further permissions questions can be emailed to **permissionrequest@cengage.com** While every effort has been made to ensure the reliability of the information presented in this publication, Gale, a part of Cengage Learning, does not guarantee the accuracy of the data contained herein. Gale accepts no payment for listing; and inclusion in the publication of any organization, agency, institution, publication, service, or individual does not imply endorsement of the editors or publisher. Errors brought to the attention of the publisher and verified to the satisfaction of the publisher will be corrected in future editions.

Gale
27500 Drake Rd.
Farmington Hills, MI, 48331-3535

ISBN-13: 978-1-4144-4170-2
ISBN-10: 1-4144-4170-3

ISSN 1094-3552

This title is also available as an e-book.

ISBN-13: 978-1-4144-4948-7
ISBN-10: 1-4144-4948-8
Contact your Gale, a part of Cengage Learning sales
representative for ordering information.

Printed in the United States of America
1 2 3 4 5 6 7 14 13 12 11 10

A Wrinkle in Time

Madeleine L'Engle

1962

Introduction

The novel *A Wrinkle in Time*, by American author Madeleine L'Engle, contains elements of both fantasy and science fiction. It was originally conceived and written as a young-adult novel, but many readers comment that the novel readily sustains the interest of adult readers and even question whether the book is truly a "young-adult" novel. The novel is the first in a series called the Time Quartet; the other novels in the series are *A Wind in the Door*, *A Swiftly Tilting Planet*, and *Many Waters*. A fifth novel, *An Acceptable Time*, turned the quartet into a quintet, yet it is still referred to as the Time Quartet.

In discussing L'Engle's work, critics also talk about the "frameworks" that organize the novels. One of these is called the "chronos" framework; the novels in this framework are written in a more or less realistic style and are all structured around a family called the Austins. In her autobiographical book *A Circle of Quiet*, L'Engle explains that chronos is everyday clock time. In contrast is the "kairos" framework. These novels sometimes have realistic settings, but they more often have elements of science fiction, fantasy, and even magic. This vision of time is God's time, where past and present are meaningless, the novels are structured around the Murry and O'Keefe families. In both frameworks, the tales deal with subsequent generations; thus, for example, Meg Murry and Calvin O'Keefe in *A Wrinkle in Time* become the parents of Polly O'Keefe, who appears as the protagonist in later books. Also, characters from both the chronos and kairos frameworks cross over into each other, creating an interlocking world where time and historical events are shared.

A Wrinkle in Time is one of L'Engle's earliest books, and it was rejected by more than two dozen publishers before John Farrar of the publishing firm Farrar, Straus & Giroux, agreed to read it. He published it not because he believed it would sell but simply because he liked it. *A Wrinkle in Time* went on to win the prestigious Newbery Medal in 1963 and has been in hard-cover print ever since it was published in 1962.

Author Biography

Madeleine L'Engle Camp was born on November 29, 1918, in New York City. Her father, Charles Wadsworth Camp, was a writer and critic; her mother, also named Madeleine, was an accomplished pianist. L'Engle was a shy, awkward child, and her teachers believed she was of limited ability, so she retreated into a world of books and writing, including a journal she began keeping at the age of eight. She had a series of governesses and attended boarding schools, including one in Switzerland and one in Charleston, South Carolina, after her family returned to the United States to settle in Florida. After graduating with honors from Smith College in 1941, she moved to New York City. There she met Hugh Franklin, an actor, when she appeared in a play with him, and the two were married in 1946. Meanwhile, in 1945, she published her first novel, *A Small Rain*. In the late 1940s, after the birth of the couple's first child, the family moved to rural Connecticut, where they lived in a two-centuries-old farmhouse called Crosswicks. But in 1959 they returned to New York City so that Hugh could resurrect his acting career. Just prior to the move, though, the family took a ten-week camping trip across the United States. L'Engle later said that it was during this trip that she conceived *A Wrinkle in Time*, which she completed in 1960.

What followed was an enormously busy time in the author's life. In addition to raising her two biological children and a third adopted child, L'Engle taught from 1960 to 1966 at St. Hilda's and St. Hugh's School in New York City. She also wrote and published numerous novels (for both adults and young adults), as well as a collection of poetry, autobiographies (in a series of four books called *The Crosswicks Journals*), and books on art and religion —a total of three dozen books in all. Additionally, she was in demand as a speaker, seminar leader, and writer-in-residence. She served a term as president of the Authors Guild, was named an Associate Dame of Justice of the Venerable Order of Saint John, directed her church choirs, and received honorary degrees from a dozen colleges and universities. She also served as the librarian and writer-in-residence at the Episcopal Cathedral of St. John the Divine in New York City for a lengthy period. Her writing has won numerous awards, including the ALAN Award and the Kerlan Award.

L'Engle was seriously injured in a car accident in 1991. In her final years, her travel schedule was limited because of osteoporosis, and she suffered a stroke in 2002. She died in a nursing home in Litchfield, Connecticut, on September 6, 2007, at the age of eighty-eight.

Plot Summary

Chapter 1: Mrs. Whatsit

On a wet, stormy night, fourteen-year-old Meg Murry lies awake in bed in her attic room, troubled by thoughts that she does not fit in with the other students at her high school and that her teachers are threatening to give her low grades because her classroom performance is poor. Worse, though, is the fact that her father, Dr. Alexander Murry (whose first name is revealed only in a later novel in the Time Quartet series), has been missing for over a year. When the family dog, Fortinbras, begins barking, she worries that a neighborhood tramp, who stole bed sheets from the constable's wife, Mrs. Buncombe, is hanging about. Meg goes down to the kitchen, where her brother, five-year-old Charles Wallace, appears to be waiting for her. Mrs. Murry (Katherine, or Kate) enters and tells Meg that she spoke with Mrs. Henderson, whose son Meg had beaten up at school that day. Meg laments that she is an oddball and wishes she were more normal, like her twin siblings, ten-year-old Sandy (Alexander) and Dennys. Charles Wallace says that he has discussed Meg's problems with Mrs. Whatsit, though he refuses to provide any information about the woman's identity.

The dog begins barking again, so Mrs. Murry goes outside to investigate. She returns with Mrs.

Whatsit, an eccentric vagrant who is bundled in wet clothing. Mrs. Whatsit explains that while she enjoys stormy weather, the storm has blown her off course. She also confirms that it was she who stole the bed sheets from Mrs. Buncombe. After drying her feet, she announces that there is such a thing as a tesseract. She then dashes off, leaving the family stunned by her odd statement. In particular, Mrs. Murry, who like her husband is a scientist, is mystified that Mrs. Whatsit knows about the tesseract.

Chapter 2: Mrs. Who

The following day is a difficult one for Meg. She is puzzled by the events of the previous evening, but her mother tells her "you don't have to understand things for them to *be*." At school, a teacher sends her to the office of the principal, Mr. Jenkins, for being rude. She bristles when the principal asks her about her home life and suggests that the family needs to accept the fact that Meg's father is gone for good. After school, Meg, Charles Wallace, and Fortinbras go to a local haunted house to visit Mrs. Whatsit. Along the way they encounter Calvin O'Keefe, a popular athlete at Meg's school who admits that he is strangely fascinated by the haunted house. The three enter the house and find Mrs. Who, a plump woman wearing large glasses and sewing with Mrs. Buncombe's sheets while a black pot boils on the hearth. Mrs. Who cryptically refers to Calvin as a "good choice." She also tells them that the time is drawing near and that the three should get food and rest. Meanwhile, Charles Wallace has invited Calvin for dinner, and the three depart for the Murry home.

Chapter 3: Mrs. Which

Chapter 3 is set in the Murry home before and after dinner. Before dinner, Meg shows Calvin a picture of her father, who used to work at Cape Canaveral but has been missing for over a year. She also helps Calvin with his math and physics, even though she is in a lower grade. Her ability in science and math was fostered by her father, who used to play number games with her. Calvin, meanwhile, enjoys the Murry family's warmth and closeness; as the third of eleven children, he feels that his parents pay little attention to him. After dinner, as Calvin reads to Charles Wallace, Meg and her mother discuss Mr. Murry's disappearance. Mrs. Murry accepts that there are some things that have no explanation, but Meg is unwilling to agree with this notion.

Media Adaptations

- A film version of *A Wrinkle in Time* was released by Walt Disney Home Entertainment on DVD and VHS in 2004. It stars Katie Stuart and David Dorfman and was directed by John Kent Harrison. Running time is two hours and eight minutes.

- An audiobook version, read by the author, was released in 1994 by Recorded Books. Running time is approximately five and a half hours.

- An operatic version of *A Wrinkle in Time* premiered in 1991. The composer is Libby Larsen, and the librettist is Walter Green.

Meg and Calvin take a walk in the yard, where

Meg tells Calvin that her father was an astrophysicist who worked first in New Mexico, then at Cape Canaveral. Calvin mentions the rumors that he has heard about Mr. Murry's disappearance, such as the one spread by the postmistress that he has run off with another woman, but Calvin reassures Meg that he does not believe the rumors. Calvin and Meg hold hands, and Meg blushes when Calvin tells her that she has beautiful eyes. Suddenly Charles Wallace appears and tells them that it is time for them to go in search of Mr. Murry. Mrs. Who appears in the moonlight, and Mrs. Whatsit, wearing Mrs. Buncombe's sheets, climbs over a fence into the yard. Then Mrs. Which announces her presence in a gust of wind but says that for her to fully materialize would be too tiring. The three are collectively referred to as the Mrs. Ws.

Chapter 4: The Black Thing

Chapter 4 takes place on the planet Uriel. Meg feels herself cast into a silent darkness until Calvin and Charles Wallace appear, along with Mrs. Whatsit, Mrs. Who, and Mrs. Which, who tell the children where they are. Calvin asks how they arrived on Uriel, and Mrs. Whatsit explains that they are able to "tesser," or "wrinkle," through space. She also tells the children that they are searching for Mr. Murry, who is facing a threat. Mrs. Whatsit then transforms herself into a beautiful creature with the body of a horse but the torso of a human. She rebukes Calvin for falling to his knees, as though he is worshipping her. The children climb onto her back and she flies over the planet, showing them green fields, a rocky plateau, and visions of beautiful creatures doing a dance in a garden to music set to words from the biblical book of Isaiah, including the famous verse "Sing a new song unto the Lord." She gives each of the children a bouquet of flowers and tells them to breathe through it if the air becomes too thin. Their travels continue, allowing them to see one of Uriel's moons. Most importantly, they see a blackness above the clouds. Meg feels the blackness, the Black Thing, as an embodiment of evil and asks Mrs. Which if this evil is what her father is fighting.

Chapter 5: The Tesseract

While Chapter 4 is dominated by images of religion, Chapter 5 is dominated by a discussion of science. Mrs. Whatsit tells Meg that her father is trapped behind the Dark Thing and that they are traveling to meet him by tessering, a mode of travel that takes shortcuts through space and time. Charles Wallace, who is a precocious boy, explains that tessering involves a fifth dimension; if the first dimension is a line, the second is a square, the third is a cube, the fourth is time, and the fifth is a tesseract, which enables them to travel through "a wrinkle in time" and space. Suddenly, the children feel themselves tessering, but Meg feels that her body is flattened and that she cannot breathe. Mrs. Which apologizes, telling the children that they are on a two-dimensional planet and that she revealing a room with machines, robotic attendants, and a man with red eyes on a platform. The children sense that he is a manifestation of the Dark Thing. He communicates with the children telepathically, without moving his lips. He tries to hypnotize them by having them recite multiplication tables, but Calvin resists by reciting the Gettysburg Address, as does Charles Wallace by reciting nursery rhymes. The man is unable to understand why they want to see Mr. Murry. He says that of the three children, Charles is the only one complex enough to understand him. He offers the children a turkey dinner, but the food is synthetic and tastes like sand. He asks Charles to accompany him so that the boy can learn about IT, and Charles agrees over Meg's protests. The Man with Red Eyes stares into Charles's eyes, and Charles becomes a different person. He appears to have been absorbed by IT. He chastises his sister for being belligerent and now claims that the food is delicious.

Chapter 8: The Transparent Column

Charles has gone over to the IT. He tells Meg and Calvin that the Man with the Red Eyes is their friend and that the Mrs. Ws are enemies. The Man with the Red Eyes identifies himself as the Prime Coordinator. He tells Meg and Calvin that Charles will lead them to Mr. Murry. As the boy leads them down a long white hallway, Meg urges Calvin to use his ability to communicate with people to talk to

Charles in an effort to reclaim him. Charles, though, continues to speak in the voice of IT, telling his companions that the Man with the Red Eyes is the Boss and that because of the conformity on Camazotz, there are no wars and no unhappiness. Charles waves his hand and a wall dissolves. Inside a room they see the boy who earlier had dropped the ball; as his punishment, he is bouncing the ball in a rhythmic fashion, but every time it hits the floor, he feels pain. In another small room, Charles shows them a transparent cylinder. Mr. Murry is trapped inside.

Chapter 9: IT

Meg tries to reach her father, but she cannot penetrate the cylinder. She attacks Charles, but her brother punches her. Calvin nearly gets Charles back from IT's clutches by quoting the lines from *The Tempest*, but Charles remains under the control of IT. Meg remembers the glasses from Mrs. Who. She puts them on and is able to penetrate the cylinder. Her overjoyed father can now see her if he puts the glasses on. By holding Meg, he is able to escape the cylinder. Charles behaves rudely to his father, but Meg assures Mr. Murry that Charles is not really himself. Charles tells the others that he has to lead them to IT. He takes them to another building, which is filled with nothing but a pulsing violet glow and a large living brain on a dais. Mr. Murry shouts to the children that they have to resist succumbing to the control of the pulsations. Meg tries by reciting the Declaration of Independence, the periodic table of the elements, and irrational square roots, but she feels herself slipping away. Calvin, sensing that Meg is being lost to IT control, orders everyone to tesser. Mr. Murry holds Meg's hand, and she feels herself caught in a swirl of tessering.

Chapter 10: Absolute Zero

Having tessered through the absolute zero cold of the Black Thing, Meg experiences a drop in body temperature and loses the ability to move or speak, but she can hear her father discussing his disappearance with Calvin. He was part of a team that wanted to tesser to Mars but somehow he wound up on Camazotz. He was in a state of despair and was in danger of giving in to IT when the children rescued him. Meg begins to regain the ability to move and speak and unfairly demands to know why her father did not save Charles. Mr. Murry responds by saying that "all things work together for good to them that love God." As he massages her fingers, Meg feels pain, which her father tells her is good, for she is regaining the ability to feel. Three creatures approach them, each with four arms and tentacles for hair. Meg is frightened, but when one of the creatures touches her, she feels warmth spread through her.

Chapter 11: Aunt Beast

Calvin tries to explain to the creatures that he is from a planet that is striving to fight off the Dark

Thing. Meg is still very weak, so the creatures take her into their care. She nestles against the furry chest of one and feels well-being. The creature rubs something over her, clothes her, and gives her delicious food. The creature asks Meg to give it a name; Meg settles on Aunt Beast. She tries to explain the concept of vision to Aunt Beast, but to no avail, for the creatures have no eyes. After a profound sleep, Meg awakens feeling refreshed. Aunt Beast explains to Meg that she and the other two creatures are from the planet Ixchel and that her planet, too, is fighting off the Dark Thing. After Aunt Beast sings her a beautiful song, Meg feels peaceful. The creatures return Meg to Calvin and her father. Meg asks whether the creatures can summon the Mrs. Ws. She tries to describe them, but again the effort is fruitless because the creatures have no eyes. To summon them herself, Meg tries to concentrate on their essence. Suddenly, in a booming voice, Mrs. Which announces the three women's arrival.

Chapter 12: The Foolish and the Weak

The Mrs. Ws join the group on Ixchel. They say that they can do nothing to retrieve Charles from Camazotz. Mr. Murry, then Calvin, offer to go, but the Mrs. Ws oppose them. Meg realizes that only she would have any chance of success in breaking through to Charles, for she was the one closest to her brother. She is terrified about having to return to Camazotz, but she is determined to try. Mrs. Which offers to tesser through the Dark Thing with Meg. Each of the Mrs. Ws gives Meg a gift: Mrs. Whatsit strengthens Meg's power of love, and Mrs. Who gives her a passage from St. Paul's Epistle to the Corinthians that empowers "the foolish and the weak," who can succeed in spite of their inadequacies. Mrs. Which's gift is to strengthen in Meg the thing that IT lacks, but Meg will have to learn what that is on her own.

Meg and Mrs. Which tesser safely to Camazotz, and Meg goes to the IT building that houses the brain, where she discovers Charles. She tries to determine the nature of Mrs. Which's gift, but Charles insists that IT has everything Meg has. When Charles tells Meg that Mrs. Whatsit hates her, the nature of the gift dawns on her: She has the power to love. She concentrates all of her love on Charles, which breaks the spell of IT. Charles runs to Meg's embrace, and the two tesser through the darkness to Calvin and Mr. Murry, who are in the garden at the Murry home on Earth. During a merry family reunion, the Mrs. Ws appear to apologize for not saying good-bye. Mrs. Whatsit starts to explain that the three have a new mission, but before she can finish, a gust of wind rises and the three women disappear.

Aunt Beast

Aunt Beast, the name given to her by Meg, is one of three creatures on the planet Ixchel who approach the travelers after their escape from Camazotz. Like her companions, she has tentacles for hair, fur, and four arms, and she has no eyes, so she is unable to understand the concepts of vision and light. She is depicted as warm and caring; she nurses Meg after she is caught in the whirlwind of tessering through the Dark Thing.

Mrs. Buncombe

Mrs. Buncombe is the wife of the town constable. Twelve of her bed sheets are stolen by Mrs. Whatsit.

Happy Medium

The Happy Medium is a jolly clairvoyant dressed in satin and wearing a silk turban. She has a crystal ball that she uses to give Meg, Charles, and Calvin visions of Earth and of the Dark Thing.

Mr. Jenkins

Mr. Jenkins is the principal of Meg's high

school. He is depicted as cold and unfeeling, and he annoys Meg by suggesting that Meg's family has to accept that Mr. Murry is gone for good.

Man with the Red Eyes

The man is under the control of IT on the planet Camazotz. He tries to absorb Meg, Charles Wallace, and Calvin by hypnotizing them with his eyes. He tells the group that he is the Prime Coordinator on the planet.

Alexander Murry

Mr. Murry (whose first name is provided in a later book) is an astrophysicist who, with a team of scientists, was experimenting with the tesseract, a mode of time and space travel. He and his team intended to "tesser" to Mars, but Mr. Murry wound up on the plant Camazotz, which had succumbed to the Dark Thing. Mr. Murry remains a captive on the planet until Meg and Charles Wallace, accompanied by Calvin O'Keefe, arrive to rescue him. At the start of the novel, no one on Earth has heard from him for over a year.

Charles Wallace Murry

Charles Wallace is just five years old, yet he is quite precocious and capable of understanding scientific concepts. He also seems to have the ability to read people's minds and know what they are thinking. Perhaps because of his raw intelligence, IT is able to capture him on the planet Camazotz, though he is later saved by his sister, Meg.

Katherine Murry

Katherine, or Kate, is the mother of four children, including Meg and Charles Wallace. She is also a biologist who works out of a lab in her home; she even cooks meals for her children using a Bunsen burner. She is also described as beautiful. Meg is almost jealous of her mother, for her mother's beauty and accomplishments seem to stand in contrast to Meg's awkwardness and homeliness.

Meg Murry

Meg is the protagonist in *A Wrinkle in Time*. She is fourteen years old and a high school student. At the start of the novel, she is awkward, shy, impatient, and sometimes belligerent. She feels that she does not fit in with the other students at school, and her academic performance is shaky, although she is very intelligent. She wishes that she could be more normal, like her siblings, the twins Sandy and Dennys. She is almost completely lacking in self-confidence. Her journey through space and time, though, changes her. Despite her fears, she journeys to Camazotz to save her father, and she willingly returns to save her brother, Charles Wallace. Along the way she is accompanied by Calvin O'Keefe, a popular boy at school, and their story contains hints of a potential love relationship between the two. At the end of the novel, Meg is more confident and self-assured, and she has learned that love is a powerful weapon against evil.

Sandy and Dennys Murry

Sandy (Alexander) and Dennys are ten-year-old twins and brothers of Meg and Charles Wallace. Unlike Meg, they are athletic and socially popular.

Calvin O'Keefe

Calvin is an older boy at Meg's high school. Unlike Meg, he is popular, and he is a gifted athlete. He is also capable of loving, affectionate relationships. Just as Meg feels that she does not belong, Calvin feels like a bit of an outcast in his large family, where he is the third of eleven children. When he visits the Murry home for dinner, he is impressed by the close, loving relationship Mrs. Murry has with her children, in contrast to his own mother, who he thinks will not even notice that he's missing for dinner. It is clear that Calvin is interested in Meg romantically.

Mrs. Whatsit

Mrs. Whatsit, along with Mrs. Who and Mrs. Which, functions as a guide, a kind of guardian angel, as Meg, her brother, and Calvin make their journey to save Mr. Murry. Mrs. Whatsit stole Mrs. Buncombe's bed sheets to sew clothing. She used to be a star, but she gave up her existence as a star to combat the Dark Thing.

Mrs. Which

Mrs. Which is one of the three celestial figures who act as guides to Meg, her brother, and Calvin as they journey to find Meg's father. Unlike her companions, Mrs. Whatsit and Mrs. Who, Mrs. Which has difficulty becoming fully materialized, so she appears as something of a haze. She also has trouble speaking, so her words have repeated letters; for example, "Nnoww, cchilldrenn, yyouu musstt nott bee frightened att whatt iss ggoingg tto hhappenn."

Mrs. Who

Mrs. Who, along with Mrs. Whatsit and Mrs. Which, functions as a guide and guardian angel to Meg, her brother, and Calvin as they make their journey to save Mr. Murry. She finds it difficult to speak using her own sentences, so she communicates largely through quotations from famous writers and thinkers.

this particular quotation as Mrs. Who's gift.

Topics for Further Study

- The tesseract is not entirely L'Engle's fictional creation. Mathematicians describe a tesseract as a kind of four-dimensional cube, and the term was first used as far back as 1888. Investigate the mathematical concept of the tesseract. Does it bear in mathematics any relationship to the concept as it is used in *A Wrinkle in Time*? Present your findings in a report.

- Read any of the ten novels in D. J. MacHale's *Pendragon Adventure* young-adult series, published from 2002 to 2009. The series is about a boy, Bobby Pendragon, who is joined by a group of Travelers to race across space and time to confront and defeat evil in the figure of Saint Dane. Prepare a chart drawing comparisons and contrasts between the novel you selected and *A Wrinkle in Time*.

- At the time L'Engle wrote *A Wrinkle in Time*, there was tremendous interest in the United States in science and especially in space travel. Prepare a timeline of key events in the history of space travel from the late 1950s through the 1960s.

- In 1960, many observers of American culture and society were becoming concerned about conformity, rather like the conformity depicted on the plant Camazotz. A key document in this examination of conformity was Sloan Wilson's 1955 novel *The Man in the Gray Flannel Suit*, a widely read novel about conformity in American business. Read Sloan's novel and prepare a chart that lists the similarities you see between Sloan's vision of conformity and L'Engle's in *A Wrinkle in Time*.

- One way of looking at *A Wrinkle in Time* is that it is an attempt to reconcile religion and science, two fields of thought that are often regarded as antithetical to each other. Research the relationship between science and religion. What do major religious groups, such as Christianity, Judaism, Islam, Buddhism, Hinduism, and others believe about science versus religion? Summarize your findings in an oral presentation.

- Using the Internet, conduct research about wormholes, or bridges in the space-time continuum that theoretically might allow time travel or travel that is faster than the speed of light. How have artists, mathematicians, and astrophysicists rendered the concept of the wormhole visually? How do they explain the concept of the wormhole? Present your findings in a PowerPoint presentation.

- In Chapter 9, Calvin quotes lines from Shakespeare's play *The Tempest* that were Mrs. Who's gift to him. These lines can be found in act 1, scene 2, of the play, and they are spoken by the main character, the magician Prospero, to Ariel. Read Shakespeare's play and write an essay on its relevance to *A Wrinkle in Time*. Explain why L'Engle used

Themes

Good versus Evil

A major theme of *A Wrinkle in Time* is the ongoing battle between good and evil in the universe. Clearly, the Dark Thing represents evil, a malevolent force that surrounds planets and stars and forces them to succumb to its numbing qualities. All of the characters in the novel are clearly identified as "good" or "bad." Meg and her family, along with Calvin O'Keefe, the three Mrs. Ws, the Happy Medium, and Aunt Beast, all represent the forces of good, of resistance to the Dark Thing. In contrast, the Man with the Red Eyes is an embodiment of the evil effects of the Dark Thing and of IT.

The Power of Love

A central message in *A Wrinkle in Time* is that love is a powerful force that humans use to combat evil. From the beginning, Calvin is impressed by the love that permeates the Murry household, in contrast to his own home, where he meets with indifference. Although Mr. Murry has been gone for over a year, Mrs. Murry sustains her love for her husband by writing him a daily letter. As the novel approaches its climax, Meg returns to Camazotz to rescue her brother, but not before Mrs. Which gives her a gift. That gift is to strengthen in Meg the thing that IT lacks, but Meg has to learn what that thing is on her own. When she encounters Charles Wallace, he tells her that Mrs. Whatsit hates her. It is then that Meg understands that the thing she has and that IT does not is the power of love. She is able to release Charles from the clutches of IT by concentrating her power of love on him.

Self-Knowledge and Growth

Meg is an imperfect heroine. Unlike the heroines of traditional romances and fairy tales, she is by no means beautiful. At the start of the novel she is depicted as shy, awkward, and homely. She is impatient and sometimes has a bad temper. She is rude to a teacher, and she gets into a fight. She feels the insecurities that are common to fourteen-year-olds. She wishes that she could be more "normal," more like the other students at her school, or more like her popular, athletic younger brothers, the twins Sandy and Dennys. She even has bad handwriting. Later, after her father is rescued, everyone tessers away from Camazotz, but Meg unfairly upbraids her father for not saving Charles from IT and the Dark Thing. By the end of the novel, though, Meg has become more self-assured. She learns from her journey that her need to conform is a flaw. She learns that her own power of loving and that the love of her family are more important than social conformity. Early in the novel she thinks, "A delinquent, that's what I am…. That's what they'll be saying next. Not Mother. But them. Everybody Else." The pronoun "them" foreshadows the pronoun IT of Camazotz. At the end, though, she is capable of thoughts such as this: "I love you. Charles Wallace, you are my darling and my dear and the light of my life and the treasure of my heart."

Style

Symbolism

A Wrinkle in Time is fraught with symbolism. The most prominent symbol is the use of light and dark. In particular, the Dark Thing is symbolic of evil—an evil that is not identified with any particular actions or behaviors. It is a presence, an entity, that surrounds planets and is capable of subduing them. IT is symbolized by the brain that is housed in the Central Intelligence building on Camazotz. The use of a disembodied brain to represent IT suggests that intelligence is not enough to lead a good life. Rather, love is a necessary complement to the intelligence of such characters as Mr. and Mrs. Murry, Charles Wallace, and even Meg herself.

Much of the symbolism of the novel is religious. The three Mrs. Ws have witchlike characteristics, but they suggest the concept of guardian angels who shepherd people through the difficulties of life. Eyes are also used symbolically. The emphasis on eyes is foreshadowed early in the novel when Calvin tells Meg that she has beautiful eyes. The Man with Red Eyes uses his eyes to hypnotize people; his eerie eyes bore into them and force them to submit to IT. In contrast, Aunt Beast and her fellow creatures have no eyes, but they have other characteristics that enable them to communicate with people. Meg is able to rescue her father by putting on Mrs. Who's glasses, enabling her to see her father; Mr. Murry is able to see Meg by putting on the glasses, and at the end of the novel he announces that he needs new glasses. All of these references to vision, sight, eyes, and glasses symbolize the notion of sight, the ability to truly see what is important and what is good.

Place Names

Closely related to symbolism is the author's use of place names. Little emphasis is placed on the New England location where the Murrys and O'Keefes live. The suggestion is that the lessons of the novel are universal, not bounded by place or time. To rescue her father, Meg first travels to Uriel, where she has visions of both good and evil. Uriel is the name of one of the archangels of biblical tradition. She then has to travel to Camazotz. This is not a name of L'Engle's invention; Camazotz is the name of a malevolent Mexican god, an evil vampire that people worshipped. Similarly, the name of the planet Ixchel is not made up. Ixchel is the name of an ancient Mayan goddess associated with rainbows and healing. It indirectly alludes to the rainbow at the end of the biblical story of Noah and the Ark, when evil has been conquered and the earth renews itself. It is an appropriate name, for it is here that the beasts, including Aunt Beast, nurse Meg back to health and restore her for her return to Camazotz to rescue Charles.

Journey Motif

Every author faces the practical problem of how to embody themes, characters, and ideas in a compelling story. If the protagonist of a story is going to grow and change, that character has to be made to confront experiences that promote growth. A common method authors use is structuring the character's growth around a journey. One of the appeals of science fiction and fantasy is that the author encounters essentially no limits in creating the journey. Boundaries of time and place can easily be transcended, and the characters can encounter magical worlds and otherworldly characters that define the experience. While an author such as Mark Twain placed his character Huckleberry Finn on a raft on the Mississippi River, L'Engle has her characters tesser through time and space, traveling to different planets, encountering magical characters such as the Happy Medium and Aunt Beast, and returning home as though no actual time has passed. Meg's journey, then, is clearly not a literal journey, like Huck's. It is a psychological and emotional journey that changes her.

Historical Context

Some readers and critics have contended that *A Wrinkle in Time* is an oblique commentary on the specter of Communism in the 1950s and 1960s. At the time L'Engle wrote the novel, the cold war between the West and the Soviet Union and its satellite countries was at its height. After World War II, the Soviet Union expanded its Communist empire into Eastern Europe. In the late 1940s and early 1950s, there was widespread fear that Communists had infiltrated American education, government, and media. In 1949, Communists assumed power in China after a long civil war, and many political observers believed that China wished to export its form of government to other Asian nations, including Korea and Vietnam. By 1960, the United States sent its first troops to Vietnam, beginning America's involvement in a long war whose goal was to stop the spread of Communism. In 1957, the Soviet Union forged a lead in the space race with the launch of the world's first satellite, and many observers were panicked that the Soviets now had the ability to deliver nuclear weapons using missiles. In 1959, the famous "Kitchen Debate" between U.S. Vice President Richard Nixon and Soviet Premier Nikita Khrushchev about the merits of Communism and capitalism took place. That same year, Fidel Castro seized power in Cuba, transforming the island into a Communist nation. Tensions increased in 1960 when the Soviets downed an American U-2 spy plane over the Soviet Union and captured the pilot, Gary Powers. Khrushchev scored propaganda points in Paris that year at a failed summit conference, pointing to the spy plane incident as evidence of American aggression.

Compare & Contrast

- **1960s:** Space travel is entirely new; the first human, the Russian cosmonaut Yuri Gagarin, is launched into space in 1961, followed less than a month later by the first American, Alan Shepard.

  Today: In spite of catastrophes such as the space shuttle *Challenger* explosion in 1986 and the *Columbia* explosion in 2003, travel in earth orbit is almost routine, astronauts live on the international space station for months at a time, and communications satellites are launched with regularity.

- **1960s:** The European Organization for Nuclear Research, known widely by the acronym of its French acronym, CERN, is formed in 1954 and begins undertaking research in high-energy physics at its massive facility near Geneva, Switzerland.

Today: CERN continues to operate, and in 1990 a project called ENQUIRE became the prototype for the World Wide Web.

- **1960s:** The civil rights movement in America is gaining momentum under the leadership of such figures as Martin Luther King, Jr.

  Today: Despite some continuing prejudice and discrimination, African Americans and other minorities have seen significant gains in such areas as housing, access to professional careers, and education.

- **1960s:** Christian religions, including Catholicism, emphasize traditional beliefs and forms of worship, though movement toward more openness and a more ecumenical spirit is taking hold, especially with the convening of the Catholic Church's Second Vatican Council.

  Today: Conflict over religion continues to exist, although earlier conflict between Christian denominations (or between Catholicism and Protestantism) has in large part been replaced by religious intolerance between Christianity, Judaism, and Islam.

All of these incidents combined to create a fear that Communism was spreading, much like the Dark Thing in *A Wrinkle in Time*. It was believed that Communism was atheistic and that it promoted a drab conformity—that it was an evil regime that had to be fought, for it drained individuality and genuine love out of people in the furtherance of its economic, political, and imperialistic goals. At the same time, it is difficult not to think of the American Central Intelligence Agency (CIA) in passages about Camazotz's CENTRAL Central Intelligence.

The CIA's involvement in espionage and the overthrowing of governments that were not friendly to the West in itself suggests a kind of conformity being imposed by a secretive, authoritarian government.

Conformity was an issue that was entering the public discourse in the late 1950s and early 1960s. During these years, the civil rights movement was gathering steam. Martin Luther King, Jr., was becoming a well-known civil rights leader, and on February 1, 1960, four African American university students broke the color barrier by "sitting in" at a segregated lunch counter in Greensboro, North Carolina. This event, along with numerous others that took place in the late 1950s, began a revolution against conformist, traditional ways of thinking that accelerated during the 1960s. Further, many social observers were concerned about the homogenization of American culture and society. For example, in the wake of World War II, many housing developments sprang up in the suburbs of American cities. One of the most famous was Levittown, on Long Island, New York, though similar developments could be found in and around most major cities. The purpose of these developments was to provide affordable housing. They accomplished that goal, but often the houses and streets were bland and uniform, much like the town the travelers first encounter on Camazotz. It was believed that these suburbs created a high degree of social conformity, with people leading similar lives, watching the same television shows, wearing the same clothes, buying the same furniture, cars, and charcoal grills, and adopting the same social attitudes—that is, living lives according the pulse that drives the lives of those under the control of IT on Camazotz.

Critical Overview

A Wrinkle in Time won the Newbery Medal in 1963, as well as the Sequoyah Award in 1965 and the Lewis Carroll Shelf Award the same year. It was also a runner-up for the Hans Christian Andersen Award in 1964. It was ironic that the novel was so well received, for L'Engle had great difficulty finding a publisher for it. She submitted the book to publisher after publisher and received in response one rejection slip after another. The chief objection to the book was that publishers were unclear what the market for it would be, whether it was a children's book or whether it was written for adults. Quoting Jean Feiwel, Jennifer Mattson notes in Booklist, "Wrinkle wasn't a book for children, and it wasn't a book for adults, and it was kind of unreal, and it just didn't fall into any existing category. So she who couldn't be classified became a class by herself."

A Wrinkle in Time was controversial, and in fact continues to be so. Many readers object to the book—and to many of L'Engle's books—because in their view the books are too religious. Ironically, though, many Christian bookstores have refused to stock the book, or any of L'Engle's books, because they object to the version of Christianity that pervades her writing. For example, they argue that L'Engle believes in universal salvation, that is, that God would never condemn anyone to hell for eternity. She also expressed doubts about her religious beliefs, and these doubts found their way into her novels. She was an avid reader of Einstein and other theoretical physicists, and she tried in her novels to reconcile science and religion, thus rejecting a literal interpretation of the Bible. Donald R. Hettinga, quoting *Dare to Be Creative*, notes in *Presenting Madeleine L'Engle* that "Mrs. What [sic], Mrs. Who, and Mrs. Which were witches practicing black magic." In *Sojourners Magazine* Suzanne St. Yves notes, "*A Wrinkle in Time* is vastly misunderstood by some fundamentalists. A well-researched book (ask any physicist) ... ended up being labeled as 'dangerous.' Angels were thought to be witches; the Naked Brain, Satan." Accordingly, *A Wrinkle in Time* has been a frequently "challenged" book, meaning that parents and citizens raise formal objections to its inclusion in school curricula or in public libraries. According to the American Library Association, the novel has consistently been on frequently challenged and banned books lists, appearing as recently as 2005.

From the start, though, *A Wrinkle in Time* was well received. The *Saturday Review* wrote: "It has the general appearance of being science fiction but it is not.... There is mystery, mysticism, a feeling of indefinable brooding horror ... original, different, exciting" (quoted by Zarin, "The Storyteller"). The reception of *A Wrinkle in Time* gathered momentum over the years, and many critics look back on the impact the book had on them, on other writers, and on readers. Jennifer Mattson, writing in *Booklist*, refers to the novel's "groundbreaking qualities" and "resilience" and concludes that "it's no surprise that the book had an impact on many contemporary writers of sf/fantasy." Writing in the *New Yorker*, Cynthia Zarin says, "*A Wrinkle in Time*, and a number of L'Engle's other books, became inextricably part of who I was. They influenced how I thought about religion and politics, about physics and mystery, and how I imagined what family life could be." She goes on to note that a college friend said, "There are really two kinds of girls. Those who read Madeleine L'Engle when they were small, and those who didn't."

Sources

Hettinga, Donald R., *Presenting Madeleine L'Engle*, Twayne Publishers, 1993, p. 16.

L'Engle, Madeleine, *A Wrinkle in Time*, Dell, 1962, pp. 11, 12, 29, 45. 92, 109, 157, 179, 188.

Mattson, Jennifer, "Another Look at *A Wrinkle in Time*," in *Booklist*, Vol. 103, No. 18, May 15, 2007, p. 58.

St. Yves, Suzanne, "Madeleine L'Engle's Search for God," in *Sojourners Magazine*, March-April, 1995.

Zarin, Cynthia, "The Storyteller," in the *New Yorker*, April 12, 2004, pp. 60 ff.

Further Reading

Hettinga, Donald R., *Presenting Madeleine L'Engle*, Twayne Publishers, 1993.

> This volume is a brief, basic introduction to the author and her works.

L'Engle, Madeleine, "Kerlan Award Lecture," in *Kerland Collection Newsletter*, University of Minnesota, Fall 1990, pp. 5-7.

> In her lecture, the author explains her efforts to reconcile science and religion and notes the profound impact Albert Einstein had on her thinking.

Tuck, Donald H., ed., *The Encyclopedia of Science Fiction and Fantasy*, 3 Vols., Advent Publishers, 1974-1982.

> These volumes form a massive reference set on science fiction and fantasy, including works, author biographies, bibliography, and information about series and interconnected works.

Westfahl, Gary, ed., *The Greenwood Encyclopedia of Science Fiction and Fantasy*, 3 Vols., Greenwood, 2005.

> These volumes update Donald Tuck's

The Encyclopedia of Science Fiction and Fantasy. Volumes 1 and 2 are organized thematically, discussing 400 science fiction and fantasy themes and putting them into historical and social contexts. The third volume contains entries on classic novels, along with films and television series.

CPSIA information can be obtained
at www.ICGtesting.com
Printed in the USA
LVHW082217130322
713357LV00013B/565